EVANGELISM UNLEASHED

RE-EMBRACING THE CATALYST OF POWER

RANDY CLARK

D0170063

GLOBAL AWAKENING

Evangelism Unleashed: Re-embracing the Catalyst of Power
© Copyright 2005 Global Awakening
First Edition, October 2005
All rights reserved

Global Awakening
1150 Lancaster Boulevard, Suite 201
Mechanicsburg, PA 17055

Unless otherwise noted, Scripture quotations are taken from HOLY BIBLE, NEW INTERNATIONAL VERSION®. Copyright © 1973, 1978, 1984 by International Bible Society. Used by permission of Zondervan Publishing House.

Note: Portions of Scripture quotations may be bolded, italicized and/or underlined for didactic emphasis.

First Printing: October 2005

ISBN: 0-9740756-3-9
ISBN: 978-0-9740756-3-1

TABLE OF CONTENTS

Introduction

The main purpose of this booklet is to create in you, the reader, a thirst to see power evangelism in our day and hour. In John 7:37-38, Jesus gave a universal call:

> On the last and greatest day of the Feast, Jesus stood and said in a loud voice, "If anyone is thirsty, let him come to me and drink. Whoever believes in me, as the Scripture has said, streams of living water will flow from within him."

My intention for writing this booklet is to educate you regarding the wonderful ministry of the Holy Spirit through the Church of the Lord Jesus Christ. I want to inform those who may not have heard the stories contained in this teaching about the relationship between the work of Jesus on the Cross and the continued works of Jesus today through the administration of the Holy Spirit. Just as Jesus represented the Father, only doing what the Father instructed, so now the Holy Spirit fulfills a similar role carrying out the instructions of Jesus pertaining to the Church and to His Kingdom.

In this booklet, I will share some stories from modern-day evangelists, and how God used them powerfully to affect their sphere of influence. I will also explain and define the different types of evangelism and show some examples of power evangelism throughout the early church (33 A.D. – 400 A.D.). I'm going to show you as well, how there have been miracles throughout the history of the Church in North America. I will conclude by sharing powerful testimonies of what I've witnessed personally in my travels around the world while preaching the Gospel of the Lord Jesus Christ. I have spoken with apostolic leaders from different countries about what God has been doing in their areas of the world. It is from this context that I write.

Having grown up in church, I was called to preach at the

age of 18. I graduated cum laude from Oakland City University, a General Baptist liberal arts University, where I majored in Religious Studies, after which I graduated with a Master of Divinity degree from The Southern Baptist Theological Seminary. I was a pastor during the 7 years of my theological training, but it was another 7 years after graduation before I began to hear the kind of stories that I will be sharing with you. I pray that these stories and examples of power evangelism, especially healing and deliverance, create in you a hunger and thirst to see the same today. If God can do it for them, then He can surely do it again in our time. Let us press in together to see nothing less that what the men and women of old saw.

Chapter 1

Testimonies of Modern-Day Evangelists

In this chapter, I want to share stories from some well-known evangelists in the twentieth century. We will look at how God has powerfully used these men and women to have an affect on the cities and nations around them. They affected their sphere of influence through a mighty demonstration of the Spirit and power, that is, through gifts of healings, faith, miracles, and deliverances.

Aimee Semple McPherson

It was the last week of April 1921:

> After that the sergeant of police assigned regular details, changed twice a day, to keep people from being trampled or crushed against the temple, where thousands were unable to gain admission. People shut out the day before would begin gathering at the doors at five in the morning. By nine o'clock the streets would begin to fill; at 12:15 the police would open the doors, and in five minutes the house would be packed. Police estimated that on several occasions 4,000 or 5,000 were turned away. (The temple's capacity was 3,000.) . . . people would stand outside the temple through an entire service. They would cling to a brick corner or ledge, in the hope that just touching the building in which God worked so powerfully must be a blessing. . . . At the end of two weeks, when the party had outgrown Moolah Temple, an ad hoc committee of ministers raised $1,500 to rent the 12,000-seat St. Louis Coliseum (with standing room for 4,000 more) for the last

week. . . . Any promoter can tell you how difficult it is to fill a hall that size today, for only one night, with or without an admission charge. Only pop stars can do it, and a few political personalities; and they require elaborate advance publicity. Before rock'n'roll only an act like Mary Garden, the soprano or Harry Houdini would book the St. Louis Coliseum for several nights-- and neither star would have risked this without several weeks of advance drumming.

Upon thirty-six hours' notice, Aimee transferred her meeting to the coliseum. The next day it was full, and for the rest of the week Aimee preached three times daily to overflow crowds of 16,000 so that the police were again called to keep people from being crushed against the doors.[1]

What was it about the meetings that drew the crowds? It was power evangelism.

William Branham

The largest auditorium in Helsinki, Finland, Messuhalli Hall, which could seat 25,000, had been rented for the meetings. The first night only 7,000 people attended, but due to the power of the gifts of the Spirit working through the evangelist, especially the gifts of the word of knowledge and healings, the attendance tripled the next night. The interesting factor was there were only 10 cars parked outside. The people were poor and had walked or ridden bicycles to the meeting.

The year was 1950 and the evangelist was William Branham. The reason for such crowds can be attributed to power evangelism that the people had witnessed at the meetings.[2]

Tommy Hicks

It was the year 1954:

The Atlantic stadium with a seating capacity of

twenty five thousand was rented. God began to stretch out His hand, even though the beginning crowds were small. The news spread rapidly; God began to heal. Before long, larger crowds were coming out to see and hear this 'miracle worker' as he was called. Ushers were soon working 12-hour-a-day shifts. Often the bleachers were occupied several hours before the services were scheduled to begin. Because of the many people who had to remain on the outside, loudspeakers were installed. Inside the stadium, the walkways were filled, then the crowd pushed down the fence surrounding the playing field and surged across, filling the field as well. They pushed down the doors of the stadium and shoved their way in.

...Because of the overflow crowds, a much larger stadium was rented - the great Huracan stadium, the largest in the country with capacity for 180,000. It had never been filled; no sports event or political rally had ever filled it. And now the little, unknown Gospel preacher had dared to rent it. The Angel had said that the wave of blessing God would send would fill the largest places with vast multitudes seeking to hear the Gospel; rulers would hear the message. Now it was literally coming to pass.

...Outstanding healings took place, too numerous to recount.... Stolid cynicism gave way to hope. Proud Argentines became as emotional as any Pentecostal. ...The lame were walking, the paralyzed set free. The blind were seeing, stretcher cases healed. Ambulances brought invalid patients and returned empty. Life and health flowed like a river, for God had come to Argentina.... An English paper of Buenos Aires reported one of the services favourably, estimating the crowds as being 200,000. It spoke of hundreds who waited from early morning for the stadium gates to open.[3]

What is so amazing about this quote is that the pastors had felt that even to rent a place that would hold 1,500 people would have been big enough. Argentina, prior to this outpouring of healing, had been resistant to the gospel as presented by the Protestants. The Protestant churches had made very little progress subsequent to 100+ years of missionary work. This healing crusade would change the atmosphere of Argentina, and prepare the way for other healing evangelists such as Omar Cabrerra, and Carlos Annacondia.[4]

Who was the evangelist? It was the American Tommy Hicks. What drew the people? It was only the power and demonstration of the Holy Spirit that the people saw flowing through the evangelist.

Carlos Annacondia

In 1984 in Mar del Plata, Argentina, Carlos Annacondia would see 83,000 people make a decision to follow Christ in response to his gospel invitations. Earlier that year he had seen another 50,000 decisions in La Plata. And in 1985 he had two meetings where 60,200 and 57,000 respectively were saved. What was it that drew so many people to Christ? The most distinctive aspect of Annacondia's ministry is the ministry of deliverance that he brings to the people after they accept the Lordship of Jesus Christ. As soon as the people's names are taken for salvation, Annacondia begins to come against the demon spirits that are in them. The spirits begin to manifest in the people, and they are taken to the deliverance tent where they receive freedom from demonic spirits.

Some of the other characteristics of Annocondia's ministry are the healing anointing, people being slain in the Spirit, and people's teeth being filled with gold and platinum. When I was in Argentina in 1998, Roberto, his former campaign manager who was now working for the Central Baptist Church, told me at one point that you had to have at least four teeth supernaturally filled to give a testimony due to the fact that so many teeth had been filled with gold and platinum. God used these phenomena to catch the interest of the press who then called attention to Anaconda's crusades. As a result of the phenomena, some of the crowds exceeded over 100,000 in attendance.

Oral Roberts

"My crusades were at full strength, all attendance records were being broken. In a single year—1957—a million souls had been won to Christ...."[5] writes Oral Roberts of his 1957 evangelistic crusades in which individual attendance sometimes swelled to 50,000-100,000. To these events the spiritually hungry and physically hurting flocked. What motivated and empowered this man of God?

> God let me know in unmistakable terms ...that I, although not some great person, carried His healing call in me, and that I, indeed was a forerunner through my preaching the anointed Word of God and seeing it confirmed with signs and wonders (see Mark 16:20).[6]

What drew the people? What contributed to the dramatic number of conversions?

> [In 1957] as I ministered in the big tent in many American cities, we had our largest crowds in any year...and the largest number of healings.[7]

The same year he lead a million souls to Christ was the year the largest number of healings occurred in his crusades as he preached the Word with signs and wonders following. What a clear indicator of the value of power evangelism where healing and deliverance demonstrate and vindicate the message of the gospel.

Lester Sumrall

In 1953 Dr. Lester Sumrall had an encounter with demons while planting a church in Manila, Philippines. A woman, Clarita

Villanueva, had been experiencing attacks and bite marks on her body from what had commonly become known as "The Thing." "The Thing" was a supernatural force that no once could see, yet there would be physical marks on her body as they attacked her. These attacks were so terrible and had the curiosity of so much of the city that they would often write articles about what Clarita was experiencing in the newspapers for the people of the city to read.

One night, while at home with his wife, Dr. Sumrall had the radio on, and heard this woman crying out and screaming while the doctors were calling it epilepsy and extreme hysteria. Lester knew that is was something different. He knew that it was the work of the devil. He could not sleep that night after hearing the screams, so he stayed up all night and prayed until morning. God spoke to his heart and said, "If you will go to the jail and pray for her, I will deliver her." But he found himself answering the Lord that he didn't want to go because scientists, professors, legal experts, and even spiritualists had been trying to deliver her without any results. The Lord told him that he wasn't sincere in wanting to see Clarita delivered because, as God said, "you refuse to go and see her."

Through some friends' connections with the Mayor of Manila, God provided an appointment for Lester to go and pray for her. Here is the story in his words.

> After we gathered in the chapel, Dr. Lara asked that Clarita be brought in. She observed each person slowly and closely as she entered the room. When she came to me at the end of the line, her eyes widened and she glared at me saying, "I don't like you!"
>
> They were the first words the devil spoke through her lips to me. The demons used her lips constantly to curse me, to curse God, and to curse the blood of Christ. She did this in English, yet after she was delivered, I had to converse with her through an interpreter, as she could

not speak English.

I had her sit on a wooden bench, and I drew up a chair in front of her. "Clarita," I said, "I have come to deliver you from the power of these devils in the name of Jesus Christ, the Son of God."

Suddenly she went into a fit of rage, screaming, "No, no! They will kill me!" Her body became rigid and she became unconscious...Taking hold of her head with hands I cried, "Come out of her, you evil and wicked spirit of hell. Come out of her in Jesus' name!"[8]

After a day of prayer and fasting, he returned the following morning to be victorious over the enemy. He again commanded the demons to come out of her and never to return. Even though the demons tried to come back multiple times, the woman was completely made whole by the power of God from that hour on. Lester recounts:

> On May 28, 1953, a headline in the *Manila Chronicle* read: "Victim of 'The Thing' Says Torturer Has Disappeared."
>
> The Thing is dead! This every believer can now proclaim as Clarita Villanueva... claimed yesterday that "The Thing" has finally been exorcised.
>
> Clarita told of her deliverance from her attackers as she pleaded for mercy before Judge Natividad Almeda-Lopez, who was to have tried her on vagrancy and prostitution charges.
>
> The girl said the prayers of American minister, Dr. Lester F. Sumrall, who purposely visited her to purge the devil, did it. Since Friday, May 22, when the minister prayer

with her at the city jail chapel for women,
"The Thing" had never appeared again,
Clarita added.[9]

It is said that this one deliverance opened up the whole city to
the gospel of the Lord Jesus Christ. What was the cause for the
heavens opening over the city? It was power evangelism – a
demonstration of the realm of God that invaded and broke the
power of the enemy's realm. It was the gifts and power of the
Holy Spirit being made manifest in a city to break it open for the
good news of Jesus to come and penetrate it.[10]

Reinhard Bonnke

In 1977 Reinhard Bonnke had 40,000 people attend the
last night of a crusade in Africa, even though just a few days
earlier there were only a few hundred who attended. What had
drawn the mass of people to the crusade? It was the report of
Jesus' healing ministry still occurring today through Evangelist
Reinhard Bonnke. He would later see even much larger crowds
– at Ibadan, Nigeria, the crowd was estimated at 500,000 by the
press, but some more conservative estimates by Reinhard's team
were about 250,000.[11] He has since ministered in Africa to crowds
of over 1,000,000 people in his evangelistic crusades.

Benny Hinn

By 1997 Benny Hinn would be filling stadiums in North
America drawing crowds of over 20,000 people in attendance.
Around the world, he would draw even larger crowds than he does
in North America. What is it about Benny's ministry that has drawn
the crowds? Nothing more than the healing power and presence of
the Holy Spirit that is extremely evident in his crusades.

People Are Drawn by Healing Power

Whether it was Aimee McPherson in the 1920's, William

Branham in the 1947, Oral Roberts in 1957, Reinhard Bonnke in 1977, Carlos Annacondia in 1987, or Benny Hinn in 1997, one thing remains the same; **people are drawn to Jesus when they see His healing power demonstrated in their midst**. It is also true that the miraculous healing ministry was a primary reason for the success of the missionary activities of those who believed and practiced healing in their ministries. "This burst of independent mission work - remarkably vital in contrast to the sluggish and impoverished mission programs of most denominations - resulted in stunning growth for world-wide Pentecostalism. The success of miracle-based evangelism seemed to Pentecostal leaders one more confirmation that God was behind the revival."[12]

There could be many more stories of men and women and their great evangelistic harvests because there are so many witnesses to these events. The most exciting aspect of "power evangelism" isn't in the stories of the past, but it is in the stories that can happen in the future. As great as the moves of God were in our past, the greatest healing movement of God, I believe, is still in our future. William Branham, Oral Roberts, Paul Cain, and Smith Wigglesworth all prophesied of a great future revival. Bible scholars Jack Deere and G.B. Caird believe that the Scriptures teach that there will be a great revival at the end of time.[13] I want to be a part of it, and I hope you, the reader, do too.

Chapter 2

Different Types of Evangelism

Now that we've seen the demonstration of the Spirit's power in some modern-day evangelists, I want to discuss with you the different types of evangelism that are understood throughout the church. I would also like to define how I am using the term "power evangelism." I want you to hear my heart as you read this. I am not, by any means, emphasizing power evangelism as a replacement for the other types of evangelism. But I believe that it is not an either/or, but it has to be a both/and. It is power evangelism coupled with the other types of evangelism that will be most effective in these days to see the lost come to the Lord.

Presence Evangelism

Evangelism is a priority for most of the Church. It is, however, understood and accomplished differently in diverse segments of the Church. Some emphasize what is called "presence evangelism." This is evangelism by being the salt and light that Jesus longed for us to be. Jesus said in Matthew 5:13-16:

> You are the salt of the earth. But if the salt loses its saltiness, how can it be made salty again? It is no longer good for anything, except to be thrown out and trampled by men.

> You are the light of the world. A city on a hill cannot be hidden. Neither do people light a lamp and put it under a bowl. Instead they put it on its stand, and it gives light to everyone in the house. In the same way, let your light shine before men, that they may see your good deeds and praise your Father

in heaven.

This is evangelism through bringing the love of God into hurting contexts, as represented by orphanages, hospitals, relief efforts, and many other similar kinds of activity. It is evangelism by people seeing our "good deeds" so that we can bring praise to God in heaven. The liberal churches would be good examples of where this form of evangelism is almost the exclusive form practiced by the church.

Presentation Evangelism

Other churches emphasize presentation evangelism. This type of evangelism is centered in the sharing of the gospel, presenting the claims of Christ, and calling for a commitment to Christ. This form of evangelism is based more upon reason and logic to come to the faith. The evangelical churches would be good examples of this form of evangelism.

Power Evangelism

Still, other churches emphasize power evangelism. This type of evangelism is connected to some ministry of power, which usually utilizes one of the gifts of the Holy Spirit, which in turn gives opportunity for the presentation of the gospel. The display of power is also seen to cause many to come to faith in Jesus Christ. **This type of evangelism would often be connected to gifts of healings, working of miracles, and deliverances. This will be the primary way power evangelism is to be understood in this booklet.**

However, I would be quick to add that during times of Divine visitation by the Holy Spirit there has been another display of power. That display is a deep conviction for sins that often leaves the person under this conviction in a state of spiritual anguish, which is a deep sorrow for their sins. This deep spiritual anguish continues until they become evangelized, saved, converted or whatever term is used in your Christian context. This spiritual anguish would be so strong that they often would be reduced to tears, sometimes weeping and wailing over their eternal separation from God. Sometimes power evangelism has been demonstrated by knocking the unregenerate to the ground, other times causing them to jerk, and even at other times causing them to tremble under deep conviction. These latter phenomena occurred during the First and Second Great Awakenings and the Cane Ridge Revival, as well as most other revivals in church history. Good examples of churches which have emphasized power evangelism at times would be the Pentecostal, Charismatic, and Third Wave Evangelical churches.[14]

Strategic Level Spiritual Warfare

Groups within all three of the above-mentioned churches also see another form of power evangelism, that being "Strategic Level Spiritual Warfare" (SLSW). The basic concept in SLSW is the need to win a victory over the powers and principalities in the heavenlies which rule over region. There is great diversity in the practice of strategic level spiritual warfare. It has been done through praise and worship, declarative prayer, identificational repentance, intercessory prayer, and prophetic dance. It presupposes that through various means God will lead the people of prayer to know strategically how and what to pray, praying not olny for God's blessing, but also for the binding of Satan. This it presupposes a power encounter in the heavenlies that affects the ability of the unbelievers in a region to accept or reject the claims of Christ.[15] Today most all of the largest churches in Latin America that I personally know about practice some form of SLSW.

One of the strategies of the enemy is to cause the Church to be divided over partial truths. It isn't that one of these forms is right and the others are wrong. The truth is that all these types of evangelism are valid forms of evangelism. Therefore, in discussing the effectiveness and potential blessing of power evangelism for reaching a post-modern world, do not hear a rejection of the other forms of evangelism. When all types of evangelism are embraced and practiced by the church in a community, the greater can be the harvest in that community.

The following material is to inform those that may be unaware today of the role power evangelism has played in the advancement of the Christian faith. Like myself, many Christians may have been involved for years in the local church, or even graduated from a denominational Bible School, Christian College, or Seminary, and still not have heard testimony of God's power working through His servants to bring many to Christ.

Chapter 3

Early Examples of Power Evangelism

We now briefly consider the presence of power evangelism from the New Testament period through the first four hundred years of the Church. You will see how power evangelism existed in the early church, though they might not have used the same terminology.

New Testament Revival: Paul in Ephesus

The greatest example of power evangelism in the New Testament is the Ephesian Revival recorded in chapter 19 of the Acts of the Apostles. Luke tells us, "This went on for two years, so that all the Jews and Greeks who lived in the province of Asia heard the word of the Lord. God did extraordinary miracles through Paul, so that even handkerchiefs and aprons that had touched him were taken to the sick, and their illnesses were cured and the evil spirits left them."[16] So many people were becoming Christians that it was threatening the economic livelihood of the silversmiths who made their living from selling the idols of Artemis.

Listen to the silversmith, Demetrius, " . . . And you see and hear how this fellow Paul has convinced and led astray large numbers of people here in Ephesus and in practically the whole province of Asia."[17] Church growth experts have said that this was Paul's greatest success, and that the church at Ephesus could have been 50,000 strong by the time that Timothy was overseeing it. It is interesting that this was also where Paul saw the greatest display of what we now call "power evangelism."

However, demonstrations of power alone would not result in effective evangelism – Paul was also involved in presentation evangelism. Luke tells us, "Paul entered the synagogue and spoke boldly there for three months, arguing persuasively about the kingdom of God. But some of them became obstinate; they refused to believe and publicly maligned the Way. So Paul left them. He took the disciples with him and had discussions daily in the lecture hall of Tyrannus. This went on for two years, so that all the Jews and Greeks who lived in the province of Asia heard the word of the Lord."[18]

Power evangelism is not the enemy of presentation evangelism; it doesn't say, "I have no need of you." Rather, from a biblical perspective, power evangelism is the best friend of presentation evangelism. It is hoped that this teaching will build a bridge between these two forms of evangelism over which evangelists of the gospel can cross and embrace each other as friends and fellow soldiers of the Captain of our Faith, Jesus Christ.

The Early Church (100-400A.D.)

The Yale Professor of History, Ramsay MacMullen, wanted to find out how the early Christians who had no political power were successful in defeating the old religions, and establishing Christianity as the religion of the Roman Empire, even though they were in fact considered practitioners of an illegal religion for part of the period 100-400 AD. His research was surprising. It was not primarily great preaching or the result of great apologists for the faith that brought this shift, but it was primarily the result of power evangelism. People became Christians because the God the Christians worshipped was more powerful than the false gods they had been worshipping before coming to Christ. This was evidenced in the power of God to heal and especially in the deliverance ministry of the Christians. The deliverance ministry was a reality in this time even among other religions. What was so different was how fast the Christians could bring deliverance to those needing it. This discovery, that power evangelism was the context for presentation evangelism to be more readily accepted by unbelievers was not the discovery of some Church historian or theologian, but rather a secular historian from Yale University.[19]

Ironically, a great English Christian named Michael Green, in his book *Evangelism in the Early Church*, which covers the first 300 years of Christianity, barely mentions the role of deliverance and healing as a means of evangelizing. This demonstrates how paradigms often prevent us from seeing what is there because we have been trained to expect to see things a certain way. This is why, often, new perspectives are brought from someone outside a particular field of study or work.

As space does not permit a thorough historical study of the role of power evangelism in the history of the Church, we move now to more recent examples of power evangelism and hear the testimonies of those leading the revivals in which it played a central role.

Chapter 4

Power Evangelism: Spiritual Awakening in Britain and America

The stirrings of nearly simultaneous spiritual renewal burned in both Great Britain and America, with each nation's revival influencing and feeding the other's. The First Great Awakening occurred during the colonial period of the United States. Its early stirrings began in New Jersey in 1726 with the preaching of Theodore Frelinghuysen to his Dutch Reformed congregation. Theodore influenced Presbyterian pastors Gilbert Tennent and William Tennent, Jr. who then spread revival among the Scotch-Irish of the Middle colonies. In December 1735 the flames intensified and spread into New England under the ministry of Jonathan Edwards.[20]

In England revival was breaking out under the ministries of John Wesley and George Whitefield. The year 1739 was to be a significant year for both.

John Wesley

According to D. Palmer:

> Encouraged by an account of the Great Awakening in New England by Jonathan Edwards and by George Whitefield's successes at outdoor preaching, Wesley swept away his ecclesiastical and High Church views and began preaching in fields at Bristol (1739). The Methodist revival in England had begun. "I look upon the world as my parish," he wrote, "Thus far, I mean, that in whatever part I am in, I judge it meet, right, and my bounden duty to declare unto all that are willing to hear the glad tidings of salvation."[21]

Various, mighty manifestations of power were a hallmark of Wesley's ministry. The occurrence of people being thrown to the ground (later called swooning and then later slain in the Spirit) happened quite frequently.

Note these accounts from John Wesley's journal:

> In the midst of the dispute, one of the ladies present felt as if she were pierced by a sword. Before she could be brought to another house, where I was going, she could not avoid loudly crying out, even in the street. But no sooner had we made our request to God than He sent her peace from His holy place. . . .[22]

> The next Saturday at Weaver's Hall a young man was suddenly seized with a violent trembling. In a few minutes, the sorrows of his heart increased and he sank down to the ground. We never ceased calling upon God till He raised him up full of peace and joy in the Holy Spirit....[23]

> Thursday while I was preaching at Newgate... I asked them to pray that if this [salvation for all men] was the will of God, He would bear witness to His word. Immediately one, then another, and another sank to the earth. They dropped on every side as if thunderstruck. One cried aloud. We besought God in her behalf and He turned her heaviness into joy. . . . In the evening I was again pressed in spirit to declare, Christ "gave himself a ransom for all" (1 Tim. 2:6) Almost before we called upon God to set to His seal, He answered. One was so wounded by the Spirit that you would have imagined she could not live a moment. But soon His abundant kindness was revealed to her, and she loudly sang of His righteousness. . . .[24]

> By the end of April, we understood that many were offended at the cries of those on whom the power of

God came. One of these was a physician who was afraid these cases might be fraud. Today while I was preaching at Newgate, one whom the doctor had known for many years was the first who broke out into strong cries and tears. The physician could hardly believe his own eyes and ears. He went over and stood close to her, observing every symptom, till great drops of sweat ran down her face and her entire body shook. He did not know what to think, being clearly convinced it was not fraud nor any natural disorder. But when both her soul and body were healed in a moment, he acknowledged the work of God.[25]

By May many more than before were offended. At Baldwin Street my voice could scarcely be heard amid the groanings of some and the cries of others, calling aloud to Him who is able to save.

A Quaker who stood by was greatly displeased at the commotion and was biting his lips and scowling angrily. Suddenly he dropped down as if thunderstruck. The agony he was in was terrible to behold. We begged God not to charge him with his folly. God answered and the man soon lifted his head and cried aloud, 'Now I know you are a prophet of the Lord!'[26]

At Newgate another mourner was comforted. I was asked to step into a house to read a letter written against me. The letter stated that I was a deceiver of the people because I taught that God wills all men to be saved. One person who had long asserted the contrary was there when a young woman came in. Just as we rose from giving thanks, she reeled four or five steps, then dropped down.[27]

These were the accounts of sinners and religious enemies and critics who were knocked down to the ground, or slain in the Spirit. Revivals often are accompanied by such phenomena. It is difficult for us to accept that God's Spirit would cause people to be thrown to the ground, but in Scripture when there is a theophany (God revealing himself), most of the time the people become afraid, sometimes they fall, and other times they tremble.[28]

Not only was there healing, shaking, and falling that accompanied the ministry of John Wesley, there was also deliverance. Wesley writes in his journal:

> On our way home, someone met us in the street and informed us that the weaver had fallen down, raving mad. The weaver had sat down to dinner but decided to finish first reading a sermon he had borrowed on 'Salvation by Faith.' While reading the last page, he changed color, fell off his chair, and began screaming terribly as he beat himself against the ground. The neighbors were alarmed and flocked together in his house. Between one and two in the morning, I came in and found him on the floor. The room was full of people whom his wife tried to keep out. He cried aloud, "No, let them all come! Let all the world see the just judgment of God!"
>
> Two or three men were trying to hold him down. He immediately fixed his eyes on me, stretched out his hand, and cried, "Aye, this is he who I said was a deceiver of people! But God has overtaken me. I said it was all a delusion, but this is no delusion." He then roared out, "Oh, you devil! You cursed devil! Yes, you legion of devils! You cannot stay. Christ will cast you out. I know His work is done. Tear me to pieces if you will, but you cannot hurt me!"
>
> He then beat himself to the ground again, his breast heaving at the same time, as though in the pangs of death, with great drops of sweat trickling down his face. We all began praying. His pangs ceased, and both his body and soul were set at liberty.[29]

George Whitefield

The greatest evangelist of the English counterpart to the American First Great Awakening, called the Great Evangelical Revival in England, was George Whitefield. He began leading this revival at the young age of 21. He was concerned about some of the phenomena he was hearing about in the reports of John Wesley's meetings. Concerning this John writes:

> On Saturday George Whitefield and I discussed outward signs which had so often accompanied the inward work of God. I found his objections were chiefly grounded on the gross misrepresentations he heard concerning these facts. The next day he had an opportunity of informing himself better, for no sooner had he begun to invite sinners to believe in Christ than four persons collapsed close to him. One of them lay without either sense or motion. A second trembled exceedingly. The third had strong convulsions over his entire body but made no noise other than groans. The fourth convulsed equally and called upon God with strong cries and tears. From this time, I trust we shall all allow God to carry on His work in the way that pleases Him.[30]

Whitefield was drawn to America eleven times. His second trip in 1739 was the beginning of a history-making influence in the spiritual life of the church in America:

> Whitefield was the leading figure in the eighteenth–century American revival known as the Great Awakening. In his first visit to the American colonies in 1738 he helped to found an orphanage in Georgia. During his second visit, beginning in 1739, his preaching set the colonies ablaze with revival. The height of his success came in 1740 during a six–week tour of New England. In just forty–

five days he preached over one hundred and seventy–five sermons to tens of thousands of people, leaving the region in a spiritual uproar, marking one of the most remarkable periods of American Christianity.

...He was one of the first to enlist the aid of laymen, thereby helping to break down the rigid clergy–laity distinction in ministry. While not despising educated and ordained clergy, he was led to emphasize piety and gifts over official sanction.... In addition, he believed that personal study was an indispensable part of the Christian life; thus was directly involved in helping to found three American educational institutions: the College of New Jersey (now Princeton University), the College of Philadelphia (now the University of Pennsylvania), and Dartmouth; and at the time of his death he was intending to begin one in Georgia.

By his successive trips to the American colonies and extensive preaching tours throughout Britain, Whitefield helped to knit into a unified movement an evangelical network of revivalism that transcended denominational barriers.[31]

The amazing thing revealed in Whitefield's journals was the repeated statements about George being weak in body, often very ill, and God coming in power with the preaching of the word. There were accounts of deliverances, but not accounts of George praying for divine healing with the laying on of hands. Healing in this phase of Protestant history was still a lost doctrine, only later to be rediscovered by the later Holiness Movement, then by the Faith Cure Movement which included Reformed, Baptist, Christian and Missionary Alliance, other writers, and then by the Pentecostal people.

When reading the journals of the Wesley and Whitefield, one can't help but think of how Jesus rebuked the Pharisees of His day for honoring the prophets of old when their actions towards Him indicated that had they lived when the prophets ministered, they would have spoken against them also, rather than to have honored them. It is amazing how we honor today those who were ridiculed and maligned during their ministries. Wesley and Whitefield would be considered "Counterfeit Revival Leaders" if they were conducting their ministry today. They would be guilty of participating in the false "slain in the Spirit movement." They would definitely be accused of emphasizing mysterious experiences with their high value being placed on the experience. They would also be accused of exaggerating the meetings. Recordings of some of their meetings would be played over the radio, especially the more bizarre would be featured – screaming, wailing, weeping, and roaring, etc. – those things that often occurred in their meetings.

Because their meetings were accompanied with enough power to cause the affections (emotions) to be moved upon by the Spirit of God, could it be valid theory, that this very phenomena was what attracted the attention of the English and American people of that day? Both John Wesley and George Whitefield record in their journals preaching often to crowds of a few thousand to 20,000 - 30,000 in a day without any amplification at all.

What was the fruit of the Great Awakening in the Colonies of America? Was it real revival or people just being caught up in esoteric experiences? Decide for yourself. "In one period of three years during the awakening, at least thirty thousand persons were converted in New England. And in the same period, at least fifty thousand persons were converted in all the colonies. When one remembers that the total population of the colonies was about two million, these numbers are no less than amazing. A similar awakening today would have to result in more than five million conversions to achieve the same percentage."[32]

Chapter 5

Power Evangelism: Revival Spreads to American Denominations

The Second Great Awakening and the Cane Ridge Revival

The Second Great Awakening began to gain steam about 1792 when God began to visit the colleges in the United States. Then in 1794 the Spirit moved ministers to join together in prayer for revival. By 1800 revival was being experienced in many churches in the United States, and this Awakening's most famous set of meetings, the Cane Ridge Revival, greatly affected American Christianity. As in the First Great Awakening, power encounters such as falling, shaking, groaning, shouting, deliverances from demons, and falling into trances were common. The Cane Ridge meetings had the outbreak of another phenomenon, what is commonly called 'the jerks.' This phenomenon could manifest in such a severe manner upon those resisting the Spirit's activity that it led to the death of one of the detractors of the revival; it is reported that he jerked so hard that his neck was broken as he was cursing the revival.[33]

You might be surprised to find out, that most major American denominations were influenced mightily by these ministries. Almost every American denomination was birthed out of an outpouring of the Holy Spirit that developed into a movement which eventually organized as a denomination. Our mainline denominations were founded on the power of God coming to change lives.

Because I often hear the phrase, "I am not concerned about phenomena, what I am concerned about is evangelism," I want to elaborate a little more about the effect of the above-mentioned revivals upon the growth of their respective denominations. How were the Methodists, Baptists, and Presbyterians affected?

The Baptists and Power Evangelism

When several Southern Baptist seminary professors of evangelism were asked by phone, "What was the greatest revival in Baptist history?" the response was unanimously, "The Shantung Revival."[34] Healing, falling (or slain in the Spirit), electricity, laughing in the Spirit, even raising the dead are recorded in "The Shantung Revival." This was a revival built upon the desire that one had truly been "born again" even though some of the missionaries realized they hadn't, and the desire to be baptized in the Holy Spirit.

Another revival which affected the Baptist was not a Baptist revival, but one in which Baptist participated, the Cane Ridge Revival. The Cane Ridge Revival began in the summer of 1801, at that time when the population of Kentucky was 221,000. With poor transportation systems, the revival that was led by the Presbyterians had 25,000 people attend at one time. What drew all those people? Obviously, it was God. But could He have used the phenomena as His strategy of advertising to get the attention of the people? They would come for the uniqueness, but then be gripped by the power of the Holy Spirit.

Cane Ridge was part of what became known among Baptists as the Awakening of 1800. The following is a Baptist account by their historian, Benedict, regarding a Baptist camp meeting.

In the progress of the revival among the Baptist, and, especially, at their camp-meetings, there were exhibited scenes of the most solemn and affecting nature; and in many instances there was heard at the same time, throughout the vast congregation, a mingled sound of prayer, exhortation, groans, and praise. The fantastick exercise of jerking, dancing, etc. in a religious way, prevailed much with the united body of Methodists and Presbyterians, towards the close of the revival; but they were not introduced at all among the Baptists in these parts. But falling down under religious impressions was frequent among them. . . . And in some cases, people were thus strangely affected when alone; so that if some played the hypocrite, with others the exercise must have been involuntary and unaffected.[35]

In two years, a local Baptist Association in South Carolina by 1802 had doubled since 1800 and had a membership of 2,084. Another association, which had 959 members in 1801, reported a membership of 3,518 in 1803. This was not sociological growth either, because this was a time of emigration out of the eastern states to the western ones. "Kentucky Baptist grew from six associations, 106 churches, and 5,119 members in 1800 to ten associations, 219 churches, and 15,495 members in 1803."[36]

What was the Cane Ridge Revival like? What characterized this move of God? Among the thousands converted was James B. Finley, who later became a Methodist circuit rider. He wrote:

> The noise was like the roar of Niagara. The vast sea of human beings seemed to be agitated as if by a storm. I counted seven ministers, all preaching at one time, some on stumps, others in wagons, and one was standing on a tree which had, in falling, lodged against another. . . . Some of the people were singing, others praying, some crying for mercy in the most piteous accents, while others were shouting most vociferously. While witnessing these scenes, a peculiarly strange sensation, such as I had never felt before, came over me. My heart beat tumultuously, my knees trembled, my lips quivered, and I felt as though I must fall to the ground. A strange supernatural power seemed to pervade the entire mass of mind there collected.... I stepped up on to a log, where I could have a better view of the surging sea of humanity. The scene that then presented itself to my mind was indescribable. At one time I saw at least five hundred swept down in a moment, as if a battery

of a thousand guns had been opened upon them and then immediately followed shrieks and shouts that rent the very heavens.[37]

Baptist revivalism was born in this revival, and it continues until this very day in many Baptist churches. Dr. Drummond stated in his lectures on evangelism at The Southern Baptist Theological Seminary, that because of this revival the Presbyterians doubled, the Baptist tripled, and the Methodist quadrupled.[38] It is interesting that the Methodist embraced the most phenomena and had the most growth at the same time. The power of these meetings was in the deep conviction, which produced some of the phenomena, and in the other phenomena that so often accompanies a move of God, like falling in the Spirit, laughing, shaking, and comatose like states.

"The word *revival* came to mean not just renewed commitment but an intensely affectionate form of religion. It meant a taste for ecstasy. The physical exercises at Cane Ridge illustrated the depth of feeling possible within Christianity. For those affected, the Spirit of God moved through the thickets and canebrakes with wondrous effects. The third person of the Trinity took precedence. People felt the power and received the gifts of the Holy Spirit. They did not always express that power in traditional ways, in large part because they knew little of earlier charismatic forms of Christianity. To many, what happened was nothing less than miraculous – the falling, the wisdom from the mouths of babes, or more magical, the people who remained in comas for days with no ill effects (the widely publicized record was nine days). As far as the records indicate, no one claimed the power of healing at Cane Ridge and the forms of 'miraculous' speech, the holy laughter or sounds from deep within the body, took a form other than glossolalia."[39] It would be another 100 years before healing and tongues would break forth upon America in a powerful way.

Cane Ridge affected not just the Baptist, but also many of the other denominations in America. But often, when God pours out His Spirit, division results. The Presbyterians would be split into two denominations due to the Cane Ridge Blessing. The Cane Ridge Outpouring was too much for some, and so it was rejected by them.

The Presbyterians and Power Evangelism

Ironically, the tradition out of which the Cane Ridge Revival began originated with the Scottish Presbyterians. Presbyterianism is not associated with "revival meetings" today, but there was a time when they were a people of revival. Actually, almost all denominations have an initial period of revival out of which they were born. The Presbyterians had a prolonged communion service which would culminate once a year and last for 3-5 days. There had been 5-6 such meetings in Scotland where the "fire fell" or where God would "light the fire again". The "wild meetings," as they were called, began in Ulster peaking around 1624. "It was in these Ulster communions that we first have reports of people fainting dead away and being carried outside in a trance."[40]

Later in 1742 the greatest revival occurring in Scottish Presbyterianism broke out in Cambuslang, Scotland. Estimates of the attendance at the meetings ran as high as 30,000 people George Whitefield had just returned from one of his trips to America, and he preached with great passion and anointing. "Small groups of people, under deep conviction, talked all the night. Whitefield preached the thanksgiving sermon on Monday, after which people were reluctant to leave. No one could estimate the number of converted. Almost every conceivable physical exercise, including falling in a swoon, afflicted some participants. The ministers deplored disruptive behavior during the services, but in spite of their appeals many cried out, even during communion, and in later interviews swore they could not control themselves however much they tried. . . . But in these three or four waves of revival, the huge rural gatherings, with all the extreme physical exercises, dismayed or frightened possibly a majority of Presbyterian clergymen. Cambuslang was the focus of much of the controversy. Within nine years at least fifty-eight books, plus endless articles, either praised or condemned it."[41]

The local pastor, M'Culloch, developed a questionnaire to defend what had happened. "The effects on the local congregation were lasting, although the revival ebbed very quickly. Conversions continued until 1748, but with annual decreases. Crimes all but ceased in the immediate aftermath, but not for long. Approximately four out of five converts remained in the church for the next decade.[42] "Cane Ridge was the next Cambuslang."[43] The sociologist of religion, Margaret Poloma, who did the survey in Toronto, which proved the good fruit of the Toronto Blessing, had her predecessor also. Cambuslang was the Toronto or Pensacola of its day. How sad it is to think of the reaction among American Presbyterianism to the Cane Ridge Revival. Since then there has been no role of the Presbyterians in revival. But, not every denomination would be hurt by the Cane Ridge Revival; one of the denominations that would benefit the most would be the Methodists.

The Methodists and Power Evangelism

John Wesley has been called the "grandfather" of the Pentecostals. His theology was one of experience. His emphasis upon a "Second Definite Work of Grace" for sanctification would make Methodism a revival movement based upon reception of the power of God. For almost 150 years, Methodism would be the movement of the Spirit par excellence in North America. But this emphasis upon power would prove to be divisive over time resulting in a split within Methodism between those who emphasized the holiness doctrine of "Sanctification" and those who downplayed it. Those who continued to emphasize the power aspect of receiving the Spirit would eventually leave and form new "Holiness" denominations, and Methodism would eventually lose its vitality.

One of the great Methodist leaders of the 1800's was Peter Cartright. He had been touched in the Cane Ridge Revival, and was soon converted and called into the ministry. During the early days of Methodism in this country, it is reported that many young Methodist circuit riders did not marry because they knew the statistics that about 50% of them would be dead prior to reaching 30 years old. Peter Cartright was one of the courageous early circuit riders; one of their most famous evangelists of that era. From his autobiography he speaks:

> "Right here I wish to say, ...when I consider the insurmountable disadvantages and difficulties that the early pioneer Methodist preachers labored under in spreading the Gospel in these Western wilds in the great valley of the Mississippi, and contrast the disabilities which surrounded them on every hand, with the glorious human advantages that are enjoyed by their present successors, it is confoundingly miraculous to me that our modern preachers cannot preach better, and do more good than they do. Many nights, in early times, the itinerant had to camp out, without fire or food for man or beast. Our pocket Bible, Hymn Book, and Discipline constituted our library. It is true we could not, many of us, conjugate a verb or parse a sentence, and murdered the King's English almost every lick. But there was a Divine unction attended the word preached, and thousands fell under the mighty hand of God, and thus the Methodist Episcopal Church was planted firmly in this Western wilderness, and many glorious signs have followed, and will follow, to the end of time."[44]

Peter had been one of the approximately 2,000 saved as a result of the Cane Ridge Revival. He came under conviction at Cane Ridge and was saved shortly afterwards. He would always have a deep commitment to the powerful ways of the Holy Spirit he first saw at Cane Ridge.

Cartwright speaks from his autobiography about the Cumberland Revival that soon followed Cane Ridge. This revival affected the Presbyterians causing a split. But, it also had an affect upon the Methodists.

> The Predestinarians of almost all sorts put forth a mighty effort to stop the work of God. ....Just in the midst of our controversies on the subject of the powerful exercises among the people under preaching, a new exercise broke out among us, called the jerks, which was overwhelming in its effects upon the bodies and minds of the people. No matter whether they were saints or sinners, they would be taken under a warm song or sermon, and seized with a convulsive jerking all over, which they could not by any possibility avoid, and the more they resisted the more they jerked. If they would not strive against it and pray in good earnest, the jerking would usually abate. I have seen more than five hundred persons jerking at one time in my large congregations. Most usually, persons taken with the jerks, to obtain relief, as they said, would rise up and dance. Some would run, but could not get away. Some would resist; on such the jerks were generally very severe.
>
> To see those proud young gentlemen and young ladies, dressed in their silks, jewelry, and prunella, from top to toe, take the *jerks*, would often excite my risibilities. The first jerk or so, you would see their fine bonnets, caps, and combs fly; and so sudden would be the jerking of the head that their long loose hair would crack almost as loud as a wagoner's whip.[45]

Regarding this phenomena of the jerks Peter tells of a large man heading a group of rowdies who had been drinking. This leader came to the meeting where

> The jerks were very prevalent. . . . . This large man cursed the jerks, and all religion. Shortly afterward he took the jerks, and he started to run, but he jerked so powerfully he could not get away. He halted among some saplings, and, although he was violently agitated, he took out his bottle of whiskey, and swore he would drink the damned jerks to death; but he jerked at such a rate he could not get the bottle to his mouth, though he tried hard. At length he fetched a sudden jerk, and the bottle struck a sapling and was broken to pieces, and spilled his whiskey on the ground. There was a great crowd gathered round him, and when he lost his whiskey he became very much enraged, and cursed and swore very profanely, his jerks still increasing. At length a very violent jerk, snapped his neck, fell, and soon expired, with his mouth full of cursing and bitterness."[46]

Cartwright's interpretation of this phenomena is worthy of noting. "I always looked upon the jerks as a judgment sent from God, first, to bring sinners to repentance; and, secondly, to show professors that God could work with or without means, and that he could work over and above means, and do whatsoever seemeth to him good, to the glory of his grace and the salvation of the world."[47]

New revivals seem to have characteristics consistent with past revivals and the introduction of new phenomena that causes interest among the general public. Often these phenomena also produce controversy and division within the churches. The phenomena are demonstrations of power—though not the primary power of healing and deliverance which are the classic signs of revival throughout church history. When Ananias and Saphira died in Acts at Peter's feet, who could not say the power of God was present. The same can be said of the day of Pentecost when the disciples were accused of being drunk. This was not because they were speaking in other languages, for I have now traveled to many countries where I did not know the language, but never once has someone thought I was drunk because I was not speaking in their language. Peter even says in Acts 2:33, "Exalted to the right hand of God, he has received from the Father the promised Holy Spirit and has poured out what you now **see and hear .**" [Emphasis added]

Phenomena have been very much a sign of the power of God in revivals. It is sad that often when the accounts of revivals are recorded, our church historians sanitize them by removing the descriptions of the supernatural dimension of the gifts and phenomena of the Spirit which manifest in the meetings. .[48] Listen to the most famous Methodist evangelist give us his appraisal regarding phenomena:

> There is not doubt in my mind that, with weak-minded, ignorant, and superstitious persons, there was a great deal of sympathetic feeling with many that claimed to be under the influence of this jerking exercise; and yet with many, it was perfectly involuntary. It was, on all occasions, my practice to recommend fervent prayer as a remedy, and it almost universally proved an effectual antidote.
>
> There were many other strange and wild exercises into which the subjects of this revival fell; like for instance, as what was called the running, jumping, barking exercise. The Methodist preachers generally preached against this extravagant wildness.[49]

Cartwright understood there was real fire and false fire in the phenomena. He understood some, like the barking, to cross the line, moving from the Spirit to the flesh. Yet interestingly, one of the interpretations I have read of this phenomena of barking was that it was "treeing the devil." In one of my readings, it was related that when this occurred there was a breakthrough in a nearby community for the things of God.

There was one reference to phenomena and Cartwright's interpretation of it as a great evil that causes me to wonder if he was correct in his interpretation of the phenomena as being evil. He tells of people falling in the meetings or in their homes and being like in a comatose state for days, sometimes as long as a week. During this time, they had neither food nor water. He writes, "... and when they came to, they professed to have seen heaven and hell, to have seen God, angels, the devil and the damned; they would prophesy, and, under the pretense of Divine inspiration, predict the time of the end of the world, and the ushering in of the great millennium."[50]

I too would be very cautious, and not encourage these prophecies regarding the end of the world, but the other visions I am not sure I would have seen as an evil, but possibly valid. I say this because prior to the great Argentine revival of 1954 a young woman named Anni fell into trances and saw God, and things in the future, things which did happen in the Argentine revival just has she had related them.[51] There was also a great revival in China among children, where the children would go into trances and saw visions of heaven; this is recorded in the book, *Visions Beyond the Veil* by H.A. Baker (the grandfather of Rolland Baker, who with his wife Heidi are leading a powerful revival in southern Africa.) The fruit of these children's visions were the salvation of many souls as they proclaimed the gospel. Children going into trances and seeing angels and heaven also happened at Metro Christian Fellowship (now Forerunner Christian Fellowship) in Kansas City where Mike Bickel pastors.[52] Furthermore, there have been "saints" in the Roman Catholic Church who had such experiences. Protestants, especially Pentecostals, have also had leaders and people who had visions or trances, though there are few reports of being out for such long periods as several days.

How prevalent were some of these phenomena during the early 1800's? Vinson Synan states, "A responsible student of these phenomena has estimated that by 1805 over half of all the Christians of Kentucky had exhibited these 'motor phenomena'" These traits were called by some, "Methodist fits."[53] How prevalent were these phenomena outside of Kentucky? Synan states:

> From Kentucky the revivalistic flame spread over the entire South, reaching into Tennessee, North and South Carolina, Western Virginia, and Georgia. In most places, the same phenomena were repeated. In some areas, another manifestation was reported in addition to those already described. In the revival that hit the University of Georgia in 1800-1801, students visited nearby campgrounds and were themselves smitten with the 'jerks' and 'talking in unknown tongues.'
>
>> They swooned away and lay for hours in the straw prepared for those 'smitten of the Lord,' or they started suddenly to flee away and fell prostrate as if shot down by a sniper, or they took suddenly to jerking with apparently every muscle in their body until it seemed they would be torn to pieces or converted into marble, or they shouted and **talked in unknown tongues.**
>
> From 1800 until the present day such phenomena have accompanied in some degree most major revivals, regardless of denomination or doctrine.[54]

Now you have seen how power evangelism, a demonstration of God's Spirit and power, helped to birth the major denominations in America.

Chapter 6

Charles Finney: A Sovereign Visitation of God

We are now going to look specifically at the ministry of Charles Finney, a man intensely visited with experiences in the power of God and who would see extraordinary signs of God's power to see people come to the Lord.

Charles Finney –A Man of Sovereign Purpose for a Day of Visitation

Charles Gradison Finney was the greatest revivalist in America of the 1800's. Dr. Lewis Drummond, my professor of evangelism at the Southern Baptist Theological Seminary, once stated that he felt Finney was the most powerful evangelist in the history of America. His biography is filled with power encounters that he had experienced and witnessed.

It has been stated that his book on Revival is too mechanical, and has no place for the sovereignty of God in it. Yet, another perspective is that Finney realized that he was living in one of those sovereign moments in history when a Divine visitation was occurring. In such periods, there is a release of great faith that God will move; that God has sovereignly chosen this time in history to pour out His Spirit.

I came to this perspective as a result of the outpouring of the Spirit in Toronto in 1994. I had been in the ministry for nearly 24 years when Toronto began. There was such a difference in the anointing during an outpouring, a revival visitation, for which I could have been misunderstood in some of my very certain statements about what God was going to do. It wasn't that I had forgotten the issue of sovereignty, rather it was the understanding that I was now living in one of those most special moments in history when God had chosen to visit His people with His presence, power, and gifts. How much more than I did Finney understand this concept of living in the "day of visitation?"

Charles Finney's Baptism in the Spirit

Finney was converted as God sovereignly moved upon his heart. He sought God in the woods for hours, seeking forgiveness and pardon. The Scripture promises regarding such pardon were of great help to him at this time. The evening of the day he was converted, he was also baptized in the Holy Spirit. Listen to his words,

> "... and as I closed the door and turned around, my heart seemed to be liquid within me. All my feelings seemed to rise and flow out; and the utterance of my heart was, "I want to pour my whole soul out to God." The rising of my soul was so great that I rushed into the room back of the front office, to pray.
>
> There was no fire, and no light, in the room; nevertheless it appeared to me as if it were perfectly light. As I went in and shut the door after me, it seemed as if I met the Lord Jesus Christ face to face. It did not occur to me then, nor did it for some time afterward, that it was wholly a mental state. On the contrary, it seemed to me that I saw him as I would see any other man. He said nothing, but looked at me in such a manner as to break me right down at his feet. I have always since regarded this as a most remarkable state of mind; for it seemed to me a reality, that he stood before me, and I fell down at his feet and poured out my soul to him. I wept aloud

like a child, and made such confessions as I could with my choked utterance. It seemed to me that I bathed his feet with my tears; and yet I had no distinct impression that I touched him, that I recollect.

I must have continued in this state for a good while; but my mind was too much absorbed with the interview to recollect anything that I said. But I know, as soon as my mind became calm enough to break off from the interview, I returned to the front office, and found that the fire that I had made of large wood was nearly burned out. But as I turned and was about to take a seat by the fire, I received a mighty baptism of the Holy Ghost. Without any expectation of it, without ever having the thought in my mind that there was any such thing for me, without any recollection that I had ever heard the thing mentioned by any person in the world, the Holy Spirit descended upon me in a manner that seemed to go through me, body and soul. I could feel the impression, like a wave of electricity, going through and through me. Indeed, it seemed to come in waves and waves of liquid love for I could not express it in any other way. It seemed like the very breath of God. I can recollect distinctly that it seemed to fan me, like immense wings.

No words can express the wonderful love that was shed abroad in my heart. I wept aloud with joy and love; and I do not know but I should say, I literally bellowed out the

> *unutterable* gushings of my heart. These
> waves came over me, and over me, and over
> me, one after the other, until I recollect I cried
> out, 'I shall die if these waves continue to
> pass over me.' I said, 'Lord, I cannot bear
> nay more;' yet I had no fear of death."[55]

The first person with whom Finney spoke after this experience
went to get an elder to help Finney because he had been so wiped
out by the power of the experience. This elder of the church was
most serious and grave. As Finney was telling him how he felt the
man fell into a "most spasmodic laughter. It seemed as if it was
impossible for him to keep from laughing from the very bottom of
his heart."[56]

Charles Finney's Ministry of Power

Finney received a second Baptism in the Spirit within 24 hours
of the first and then began to preach the day after his conversion.
He was immediately successful in leading people to the Lord. He
would have many baptisms in the Spirit throughout his lifetime.
His ministry would see thousands falling under the power of
the Holy Spirit, healings, deliverances, shakings, groaning, and
weeping. Some of those who fell under the power of the Spirit
would not be able to get up for long periods of time. Finney would
also be used to bring about 500,000 people who had been lost into
the Kingdom of God.

Finney, like present day evangelists and pastors, had threats
made against his life. One man attended the meetings to attempt
to kill him, but being knocked out of his seat and brought under
deep conviction, he was converted to Christ instead! Like Peter
Cartwright, the Methodist evangelist before him, Finney also had
a man who greatly opposed the revival and was struck down by
God as he was drinking and ridiculing the work of God. Such
judgments of God were used to bring a healthy respect for the holy

things of God into the meetings, and they occurred more than once in Finney's meetings.[57]

There appears to have been a strong connection between the prayer ministry in his life – the way he moved the churches to pray in faith along with the prayer ministry of both Father Nash and Abel Clary – and his evangelistic success. Finney writes of Abel Clary:

> The first I knew of his being in Rochester, a gentleman . . . asked me if I knew a Mr. Abel Clary, a minister. I told him that I knew him well. "Well," said he, "he is at my house, and has been there for sometime, and I don't know what to think of him." I said, "I have not seen him at any of our meetings." "No," he replied, "he cannot go to the meeting, he says. He prays nearly all the time, day and night, and in such an agony of mind that I do not know what to make of it. Sometimes he cannot even stand on his knees, but will lie prostrate on the floor, and groan and pray in a manner that quite astonishes me." I said to the brother, "I understand it; please keep still. It will all come out right; he will surely prevail."[58]

I wonder if Nash and Clary were not breaking open the heavens over the cities and towns where Finney was ministering. I have a strong suspicion that they were doing strategic level spiritual warfare 150 years before the term would become popular.

We should desire nothing less than what Charles Finney had! Perhaps the reason that so many gave their lives to the Lord through his ministry resulted from both the number and intensity of power encounters that he had with the Holy Spirit. Let us hunger and thirst for the same degree of anointing – and even more!

Chapter 7

Power Evangelism: The Pentecostal Revival Challenges the Church

The Rapid Rise and Growth of Pentecostal Power

The 1900's entered—like the 1800's— in revival. The Frontier Revival or the Second Great Awakening, as it was called, with Cane Ridge being the most powerful of the meetings, was followed by this even more powerful revival. The Pentecostal Revival which dates back to January 1901. Again, we see people falling, shaking, rolling, weeping, wailing, dancing, laughing in the Spirit, and speaking in tongues. The uniqueness of this movement is that for the first time tongues would be tied to the baptism of the Holy Spirit as the initial evidence of being filled. Azusa Street would occur in 1906 and the first name for the Azusa Street Revival was the "Los Angeles Blessing."[59] Hungry people would travel from every inhabited continent to find more of the manifest presence of God and then return to spread the Pentecostal revival in their country. The Pentecostal revival would be characterized by its emphasis upon the return of the spiritual gifts of 1 Corinthians 12 including the "sign gifts" of tongues, interpretation of tongues, prophecy, working of miracles and the gifts of healings.

It is disappointing to me how much prejudice there still is in the church towards Pentecostals. When I was taking a course on evangelism in seminary, we studied every revival in North American church history except two, the Pentecostal Revival and the Latter Rain Revival, which was a Pentecostal revival in its origin. When you consider that the most successful part of the church in reaching the lost this century is the Pentecostal movement, it is shameful for its lack of mention in the evangelism classes of our evangelical seminaries and colleges. It is not healthy to allow our prejudice to blind us to the facts of how powerfully God has used Pentecostals to reach more lost than any other part of the church, who in the early days were poor with no institutions, buildings, money, or programs. They reached more than the Reformed, the Lutheran, the Anglican, the Baptist, the Methodist, and the Roman Catholic denominations. These denominations with all their history, buildings, finances, organization, and programs were surpassed in evangelism by the Pentecostals. What is the cause? The Pentecostals embraced the outpouring of the Holy Spirit's power, and the restoration of the power ministries of the Holy Spirit, which are often referred to as the sign gifts – prophecy, tongues, interpretation of tongues, healing, and working of miracles – as still for today. It was their understanding that the word for salvation includes not only the saving of the soul, but also deliverance from demonic influence or attack, and physical and emotional healing that gave such spiritual power to the Pentecostal message.

Most revealing is the challenge to the Church presented by the success of the Pentecostal message, a challenge well articulated by prophetic voices from what some would consider the most unlikely of sources.

Ralph Martin: A Roman Catholic Leader Speaks Prophetically to the Church

In *The Catholic Church at the End of an Age: What the Spirit is Saying,* one of the most powerful, honest books I have read, Ralph Martin compares his denomination with Pentecostals. He notes that by 1982, the Pentecostal churches (not including the charismatic who had remained in traditional denominations) had become the largest body of Protestants; larger than the Baptists, Anglicans, Presbyterian or Methodist churches. This was even more surprising when you consider that while the mainline Protestant churches had a history of about 400 years, the Pentecostals' history was, at the time, only about 80 years in duration. Only the Roman Catholic Church has had a larger following.[60] Martin, further notes that

> "By 1992 the numbers of Pentecostals
> and charismatic had grown to over 410
> million and now comprised 24.2 percent of
> world Christianity. . . My research has led
> me to make this bold statement: In all of
> human history, no other non-political, non-
> militaristic, voluntary human movement
> has grown as rapidly as the Pentecostal-
> charismatic movement in the last 25
> years."[61]

After Ralph Martin charts the phenomenal growth of the previous
decade of the Pentecostal-Charismatic in contrast to the growth
of the Roman Catholic and historic Protestant denominations,
and after documenting the decline of the influence of the Catholic
Church in society, he makes the following powerful, insightful
statement:

> [T]here is a message to which we need to pay attention.
> That message, in its simplest form, perhaps could be stated
> like this: *When Jesus is proclaimed clearly and confidently,
> in the power of the Holy Spirit, many more people come to
> faith and there is much more growth to the Church than
> when he is not.*[62]

I would hope that other denominational leaders would be as honest
in recognizing the reality of his warning, and that they would press
their movement or denomination into also asking, "Why have the
Pentecostals, who are the primary exponents of power evangelism
been so successful?"[63]

I have read few books in which there are such a spirit of
repentance as in Martin's book. Oh, how I wish other churches
had prophets who spoke so clearly to them. Listen to the closing

summary of chapter 5 "The Church, Repentance and Faith",

> "What might the Spirit be saying to the Catholic Church? A message as old and new as the day of Pentecost: Repent, believe, and you too will receive the gift of the Holy Spirit (Acts 2:38). Let us repent of any ways in which we have narrowed God, or limited him, in our thoughts, words, or actions. Let us repent of any ways we have obscured the central place of Jesus and put secondary things in his place. Let us repent of that 'ecclesio-centrism' that puts the Church in the place of Christ. Let us repent of any ways we have grieved the Holy Spirit and through our pride or fear resisted his workings."[64]

If the Roman Catholic Church has a lot more people in it with Ralph Martin's spirit, then I believe that it will see a great revival and become a prominent figure in the coming harvest. What is the prophetic voice of Ralph Martin saying not just to the Roman Catholic Church, but also to the Church at large? The harvest is upon us now, and we do not have time to continue as we have been. We must humble ourselves, and repent of our wrongs—within our own group's expression of and service to Him as the Body of Christ. And finally, we must embrace the fullness of the person and ministry of the Holy Spirit and the complete, unhindered expression of His gifts.

> "The church is a bride, and she shows to the world that her spouse is alive by living by his power and receiving life from him. **There is a danger in our day that the church will look more like a widow, alone and without resources except those possessed by any human organization**. If

we yield to what the Lord has poured out upon us
- his Spirit- the world will know that the church is
truly the spouse of a living Lord."[65]

I agree with Ralph, and I want to honor him as a prophetic voice to both the Roman Catholic Church and to the Church as a whole. Yet Ralph is not the only prophetic voice from God speaking to us today from places unexpected by evangelicals and Pentecostals.

Harvey Cox: Fire From Heaven

Harvey Cox spoke and wrote in the 60's what he thought was predictive, but time proved him to have been wrong. On the back of his new book, *Fire From Heaven: The Rise of Pentecostal Spirituality and the Reshaping of Religion in the Twenty-first Century,* Harvey Cox is identified as the "Victor Thomas Professor of Religion at Harvard University" and "the author of more than ten books, including the best-selling classic, *The Secular City."*

The irony is that the predictions made in *The Secular City* failed to materialize. The culture of the world has not become more secular, rather it has become more spiritual, though not always more Christian. Post-modern thought has rejected the closed worldview of the secular city and has embraced a worldview closer to that of the first century than probably any other century in the last 500 years. While *Fire From Heaven* is Cox's admission of having been wrong, it is more than that. Where the *Secular City* predicted that Christianity would not be able to hold the city— causing the growing metropolises to become increasingly more secular, *Fire From Heaven* is his study of why Pentecostal and Charismatic churches have thrived in the urban context. When the *Secular City* was written Harvey Cox was noting the demise of the institutional church in the changing neighborhoods of the city, and noting the death of large older mainline churches. He concluded that the Church would lose the cities of the world. He did not foresee how God would raise up out of weakness the Pentecostal and Charismatic movements, and through their weakness reveal

His strength, thus recapturing the urban areas.

Let us close this chapter by allowing Harvey Cox to speak for himself:

> THE SIGNS AND WONDERS that appeared at Azusa Street and in the global movement it loosed included far more than speaking in tongues. People danced, leaped, and laughed in the Spirit, received healings, fell into trances, and felt themselves caught up into a transcendent sphere. In retrospect, we can also describe the revival as the principal point in western history at which the pulsating energy of African American spirituality, wedded by years of suffering to the Christian promise of the Kingdom of God, leaped across the racial barrier and became fused with similar motifs in the spirituality of poor white people. It marked the breaking of the barrier that western civilization had so carefully erected between the cognitive and the emotional sides of life, between rationality and symbol, between the conscious and unconscious strata of the mind. In this context, the mixing of the races was not just an early equal opportunity program. It had powerful archetypal significance as well. It presaged a new world in which both the outer and the inner divisions of humankind would be abolished, and it was the harbinger of one of the great surprises of the twentieth century, the massive and unanticipated resurgence of religion in a century many had thought would witness its withering away.[66]

Chapter 8

A World Tour of Church Growth and Power Evangelism

We are to be passionate about world evangelization—the throb of the Father's heart of love for the lost multitudes. In this chapter I want to share stories from my personal travels around the world and take you on a tour of the continents to reinforce the relationship between signs and wonders and the growth of His Church. Where the greatest signs and wonders are being manifested, the church grows the fastest. Demonstrations of power, especially in healings and deliverances, draw multitudes to Christ

Africa

On the continent of Africa, there are over 5,000 independent Christian denominations, all born in the 20th century, and all of Pentecostal spirituality. They are growing faster than Islam, twice as fast as the Roman Catholic Church, and three times as fast as the non-Catholic and non-Pentecostal churches. In **South Africa**, they embrace 40% of the black population, in **Zimbabwe** 50% of all Christians, and "by the year 2,000 these churches will include more members in Africa than either the Roman Catholic Church or all the Protestant denominations put together."[67] The largest church in the world isn't pastored by David Yonngi Cho; it was founded by Simon Kimbangu. He started his church in 1921, and today it has over 8,000,000 members.[68] He was imprisoned because of the success of this work, and he spent the last 30 years of his life in prison. The church grew faster after his imprisonment than before.

Why have these churches been so successful is a complex question, but if you ask what one factor drew the people to first attend one of these churches, the answer is healing. "Kofi Appiah-Kubi is a Ghanaian who has written extensively on the new Christian churches of Africa. . . . Most of all, these indigenous Christian churches provide a setting in which the African conviction that spirituality and healing belong together is dramatically enacted. **The typical disciple comes to such a church for the first time in search of healing,** usually for a malady that has resisted either traditional or modern medicine or both."[69]

In the early 1990's I had Pastor Dion Robert, from Abidjan, **Ivory Coast** to come to St. Louis to speak for me. His church at that time numbered over 20,000 people and was still growing rapidly. His ministry is noted for its signs and wonders, healings, miracles, and deliverances. I believe it is perhaps the largest church in the Franco speaking world. It too, is a cell church that teaches the people in the cells to expect to see the miraculous. They had a cell of teens that prayed for a dead person who was brought back to life. Today the church runs over 100,000.

Europe

England is an example of what is occurring on the continent of Europe. A survey on what happened in the growth of the churches between 1985 and 1990 indicated that the Baptists, Methodists, Presbyterians, Anglicans, and Roman Catholics had all lost members in the United Kingdom. The Catholics and the Anglicans had the greatest losses down by 10% in five years. During the same time frame, the independent churches comprised mostly of Pentecostal and Charismatic churches, had grown by 30%.[70] It is interesting to note that the largest average attendance and fastest growing Anglican Church in England is Holy Trinity Brompton, which is very open to the ministry of the Holy Spirit, believes in healing and deliverance, and was powerfully touched by the Toronto Blessing. At one point in 1994, the lines were so long to get into the church that tickets were given out to allow people to get into the church. Recently while in England, I saw a television report about the largest church in England that was predominately black and Pentecostal in practice. It is clear that the people are hungry for a God who is seen to have power to help them in their needs.

When I was meeting with the church planting groups in **European Russia**, in Moscow, almost everyone of the major successful church planting groups were excited about and open to healing and deliverance. We went back months later to do a conference on healing and deliverance, cell group ministry, and contemporary worship. There were many healings, and when we went back a year later, we heard more testimonies of healing from those young church planters. Power evangelism is working in Europe. In almost all of Scandinavia, the largest churches are those that embrace signs and wonders, healings, miracles, deliverances, and the gifts of the Spirit.

Asia

On the continent of Asia, the largest churches in most of the nations are Pentecostal or Charismatic. The Full Gospel Church pastored by David Yonngi Cho in **Korea**, has over 800,000 members. It is the world's largest church when understood as a single congregation meeting in one place. Others in Africa are larger, but instead of multiple services in one building, they have multiple locations throughout the city or country. Healing has always played a major role in Cho's church. Spiritual warfare through prayer has also been a key factor in the success of this church[71]

In **Thailand**, Dr. Kriengsak has founded the largest church in the nation and has planted over 100 churches, in one of the most gospel resistant countries of the world, the Hope of Bangkok Church. The church has over 6,000 members in a country that professes only 60,000 Christians, but on a given Sunday only about 20,000 attend church.

Thailand has a population where 95% profess to be Buddhist, and 4% profess to be Islamic; yet in this gospel resistant country the Hope of Bangkok Church is growing rapidly. His church is committed to cell groups, friendship evangelism, expository preaching, church planting by teams, and the supernatural ministry of the Holy Spirit. "One of the outstanding features in the ministry of Dr. Kriengsak and the Hope of God movement, has been the seal of approval the Holy Spirit has given in the realm of the miraculous. . . . The gifts of the Spirit most evident in Kriengsak's life were the word of knowledge, and gifts of healing and miracles. . . . Through zealous friendship evangelism and active advertising, special events are always well attended, but as the people have seen miraculous healings take place, there has been a greater openness to hearing the preaching of the gospel that followed."[72] Like Omar Cabrerra and Carlos Annacondia of Argentina, Dr. Kriengsak believes the time he spends in prayer prior to major evangelistic campaigns has a tremendous affect upon the level of the supernatural he sees in those meetings.

In **Singapore**, Dr. Lawrence Kong pastors one of the largest Baptist Churches in the world. It too is committed to cell groups and has planted many other churches. It is also committed to allowing the ministry of the Holy Spirit to occur in their services and cell groups. Also from Singapore is an Anglican Church that runs in the thousands. It is Anglican by denominational affiliation, but it is open to the gifts of the Holy Spirit and the ministry of healing and deliverance, which is the heart of power evangelism. This church is, *The Church of Our Savior,* whose vicar is Rev. Derek Hong, and where the Bishop Most Reverend Moses Tay is stationed. I have ministered personally in this church, and know the strong desire in Rev. Hong to see an increase in the power of God to heal the sick is very evident.

By far the fastest growing churches on the sub-continent of

India are those churches that are open to healing and deliverances. One church that began in Bombay now has scores of thousands who belong to it. This is a church made up of house churches of which Pastor Joseph is the leader.

The great impact of power evangelism was evident in January-Februrary 1995, when Global Awakening took a team to the Indian cities of Ongole and Nellore in an area of India which had just been severely hit by the tsunami. Working with India Christian Ministries, the team saw the voracious spiritual hunger and desperate need of the people. It was conservatively estimated that during the 10 days out of a total attendance estimated at 350,000, that 210,000 were healed and 142,000 were brought to salvation in Christ. Predominant were the extraordinary miracles and healings that broke through the cultural and religious barriers. Many came to salvation in Jesus through the demonstration of the kingdom of God where the blind, deaf, lame, and those with tumors were being healed in the Name of the Lord Jesus Christ!

Australia

It is the same on the continent of Australia. The Pentecostals with their openness to power evangelism are the fastest growing church movement on the continent. I spoke in Sydney, Australia at the New Life Church, an Assembly of God church where Frank Houston was the pastor. His church has planted daughter churches all throughout Sydney. They run over 2,000 on Sunday mornings, but if you include the daughter churches, the attendance of Assemblies in Sydney would be over 10,000 – all of which would be the result of Frank's ministry. Frank is a lover of the supernatural. When I was there, he wanted me to speak on healing, which I did. The atmosphere was full of faith and scores of healings occurred as well as scores of deliverances.

Ralph Martin includes some statistics for Australia decadal

growth rates from 1976 through 1981: the United Church -10%, Anglican 5%, Churches of Christ 8%, Lutheran 10%, Roman Catholic 24%, Baptist 24%, Pentecostal 385%. By far, New Zealand for the period 1971-1981 was the worst: Methodist -19%, Presbyterian -11%, Anglican -9%, Roman Catholic 2% Baptist 6% Associated Pentecostal 150%.[73]

South America

On the continent of South America, I can speak from personal experience. In 1997, I went to Santiago, **Chile** where I visited the Templo Centro Metropolitano, pastored by Fernando Chaparros. It was over 10,000 people and was the second largest church in the nation. It was only a few years old, and had goals to be 15,000 by the end of the year. This was a church that emphasized healing and deliverance, pastored by a former police officer. When I ministered there, we saw many healings and deliverances. We were there to train more on the healing and deliverance ministry, and to bring renewal.

Roger Cunningham, a Vineyard pastor who loves power evangelism, told me while I was visiting him in Chile that he had been working most of his time the past year with the Baptist Churches of Chile who were hungry to learn more about power evangelism.

In 1997, I spent two weeks in South America in Chile, Argentina, and **Uruguay**. During the 14 days we were there, we saw about 2,000 healed, hundreds saved, and scores delivered. One of Omar's churches in the city of Cordoba met in an old barn like building for the meetings. We saw 800 people give testimony to being healed in one meeting, including a woman who had been blind for three years due to retina being destroyed from diabetes. The night before another woman was healed of deafness and blindness on one side of her head. The pastor told me if we could stay, the crowds would grow to over 10,000. I made a mistake and left to honor other commitments, but I wish I had stayed. Most of the time was spent ministering in Omar Cabrerra's church that is over 80,000 and meets in over 200 congregations in many cities in Argentina. His churches were the easiest churches I have ever ministered in for healing, until I went to Brazil and the Ukraine. They had been founded on Omar's healing and miracle anointing; the people understood the word of knowledge's relationship to healing, and were full of faith.

While in **Argentina**, I met the co-pastors of the Central Baptist Church of Buenos Aries, Drs. Pablo Deiros, and Carlos Mrarida. Since the visitation of the Spirit in their church, it has seen more church plants and people go into the ministry during the last four years than the church had sent out in over 100 years preceding the visitation of the Spirit. It is important to note that the visitation was characterized by falling, laughing, shaking, healing, and deliverance. Their church was the second church in the city to receive the fresh anointing of the Holy Spirit.

Dr. Deiros told me that about 70% of the Baptist churches in Argentina were now embracing the ministry of healing and deliverance. Victor Lorenzo, son of Eduardo Lorenzo, a most influential leader among Baptists in Argentina, told me that the Baptist had to move from their former opposition to the gifts of the Spirit or they were going to lose their people to the Pentecostals.

The Iglesia Rey de Reyes (King of Kings Church) pastored by Claudio Freidzon grew from 6 to over 8,000 after God anointed Claudio, an Assembly of God pastor, with a fresh anointing for healing and power evangelism. I have both visited and preached in his church. It has an atmosphere of expectation for the presence of God to visit the church and touch the people with healing, deliverance, and refreshing anointing of joy and peace. The phenomenon of being slain in the Spirit is very common in this church.

I visited and spoke in Guillermo Prein's church in Buenos

Aries as well, that has an attendance of over 3,000. It was founded by having healing and deliverance meetings in a very dangerous park in the city. Now they have meetings 21 times per week, even a service at 3:00 a.m. for the Taxi cab drivers. This church has the reputation of the most healings occurring during their services. The interesting phenomenon is that over 60% of them occur when the children 12 and younger pray for them. While waiting for the Sr. Pastor to arrive, I met another pastor whose only job was to verify the miracles. I asked this associate, "So what do you do?" He said, "My job is to verify the miracles." I asked, "What else?" He responded, "My job is to verify the miracles." One of the verifications that they have is of a woman, who had a hysterectomy, she was prayed for by the children, and now she has given birth to a child. She received a creative miracle!

Pastor Michael Richardson received his D.Min. degree from Fuller Theological Seminary. His dissertation was on the Argentine Revival. I heard him share that from the Argentine Revival a new theology came into being relating to strategic level spiritual warfare. This practice is common among both Pentecostal-charismatic churches and non-Pentecostal-charismatic churches. SLSW is another form of power evangelism. Some would say it has been foundational to the success of the Argentine Revival. Because of the success in SLSW, there are more healings, miracles, deliverances, and salvations than if they don't do SLSW.

In **Uruguay**, a country that had not had a Protestant church grow past 500, I met Pastor Jorge Marquez who pastors a church in Montevideo. The church, only being a few years old, had 3,000 people in attendance. When I asked him how he had planted the church and why it had been successful in reaching the masses he told me that through advertising it had been built on promising healing and deliverance. They were able to deliver on that promise. He had almost had a physical breakdown from the late night deliverances he had done. There were now six young pastors helping him with the 28 preaching services per week. All of who had been addicted to drugs and/or alcohol, and needed deliverance when he first met them. He also told me that key Baptist leaders were also very open to the ministry of signs and wonders in Montevideo. Jorge, had been an architect and who left his profession in Argentina to start the church in Montevideo. He had been discipled in Hector Giminez's church that had an attendance of over 100,000 when Jorge was a member. This church at that time ran services 23 hours per day 7 days per week.

Brazil is a nation powerfully affected by power evangelism. The Assemblies of God denomination is growing rapidly and numbers from 11 to 15 million members. Though it is one of the largest Pentecostal denominations, it is only one of hundreds of new Pentecostal denominations. I personally have ministered in the largest Baptist Church in the nation, the Lagoinia Igrasia Batista, in Belo Horizonte. This Baptist Church has over 30,000 members and is the mother church of a new association of Baptist churches that is growing much faster than the older Baptist Association that was begun by missionaries from the Southern Baptist denomination of the United States. The pastor believes and practices strategic level spiritual warfare, has a strong emphasis on healing and deliverance, a strong ministry to the poor, and is involved in the cell ministry that is so prominent in Brazil. There are other churches, which are fast growing, that began as Baptist but are no longer Baptist today.

Apostle Hene Terre-Nove pastors the fastest growing church in Brazil, which is the largest church in Brazil. This church was running 21,000 members when I first ministered in it and three years later (2003), it was running 48,000 members. It used to be called the First Baptist Church of Manouse, but it was disfellowshiped from the traditional Baptist Association 10 years ago when it had 700 members; now its name is Restoration.

Two years ago, I ministered in a very poor small traditional Baptist church in the city of Maua, Brazil. The power of God to heal and deliver was present. Two years later when we returned to the city we were shocked to find out the small Baptist church was now the largest church in the city. It had grown from a few hundred to over 3,000 people in two years. It had embraced renewal (Toronto Blessing), healing, deliverance, and had changed to the G-12 cell system. It had also been disfellowshiped from the traditional Baptist denomination, and was now part of the G-12 movement that is overseen in Brazil by Apostle Hene Tere-Nove.

The Baptist denomination is not the only denomination affected by the recent renewal called the Toronto Blessing. (In order to put things in perspective the reader needs to understand that I went to see Rodney Howard-Browne, not to laugh, but to receive a new impartation for healing. I did this because after asking my personal friend about the fruit in his life after being ministered to by Rodney, he told me that he had seen more healing since the two weeks being ministered to by Rodney, than he had seen in the previous nine years). The largest Anglican Church in Brazil is in Receife, Brazil. The pastor, Paulo Garcia, a graduate of Trinity Evangelical Seminary, in Deerfield, Illinois, told me that he was so touched in Toronto that he received back his first love for Jesus. His church was seeing 50 saved every Sunday, 200 more saved every six weeks after a small group experience, and the church, which was the Cathedral for the Anglican denomination in the city, had also planted 12 other mission churches since his being touched in Toronto. We were invited in to teach on healing, deliverance, and renewal.

I was invited to preach in a new denomination, Videra in the year 2000. When I then ministered in the mother church of this new denomination all heaven broke loose. Many were healed. The church had already been a fast growing church utilizing a concept of "The Church in Cells," which is much more than a church with cells. In three years the church had grown to 3,000. But, in the next two years, it grew to 8,000. In September 2003, the church's goal was to baptize in the center of the city in an open baptismal swimming pool in the public square 3,000 new converts. They had fasted, prayed, worshiped, and believed for 3,000 souls to be added. They reached their purpose by baptizing 3,000 in one day.

When I asked them the fruit of our ministry in the life of the church the pastoral staff responded, "Before you came we were a strong, good church noted for its teaching ministry, but we were not a balanced church. We had the word, but we did not have the appropriate emphasis upon the Spirit. That is why we had you come and train us. Before you came, we almost never saw anyone healed. During the last year since you came we have not had a Sunday go by without someone being healed, we have not had a week go by without someone also being healed in one of our cell groups. Our church has been changed." The last time I ministered in this church (September 2003) we saw 7 blind people healed in one night. I only prayed for one of the seven, the other six were prayed for by members of my team and members of the church's ministry team, which we had trained the year before. One member of my team prayed for three of those blind that night who were healed, and the pastor, Aloisio prayed for two of them. These were the first blind people he had ever prayed for in his life who were healed.

During the last several years, we have seen over 70,000 healings in our meetings in Brazil. It is a nation on fire with revival. C. Peter Wagner said that the epicenter of revival has switched during the past few years from Korea to Brazil. Every church that I am aware of that is growing rapidly has strongly embraced the ministry of healing and deliverance.

This rapid growth of the Church in Brazil stems from the ministry of two men who brought the Pentecostal message to Brazil at the early part of the 20th century. Today scholars believe there are more Pentecostals at church on Sunday than there are Roman Catholics attending mass.

A similar picture is emerging all over Latin America. In his book, *Is Latin America Turning Protestant?* David Stoll pulls together statistics from a number of sources to show that non-Catholic Christianity is growing in many of the continent's countries at five or six times the rate of the general population. If the statistics in Brazil are any indication, 90 percent of this non-Catholic increase is Pentecostal. Stoll predicts that if current rates of growth continue, five or six Latin American countries will have non-Catholic – mostly Pentecostal – majorities by 2010. In several other nations, the non-Catholic percentage of the population will have reached 30-40 percent.[74]

Colombia is the ripest nation for revival in the Western Hemisphere in my opinion. I consider myself a God Chaser.[75] But, while I was in Argentina meeting with leaders of the revival, I was told by one of the leaders that the real revival is in Colombia, "Where they are still killing the pastors." One of the leaders of an apostolic network of churches in Colombia later attended one of our meetings in Harrisburg, Pennsylvania. There he went through a deliverance and experienced a powerful new anointing of the Spirit. He invited the pastor to come to Colombia and myself, but I couldn't go. Pastor Charles Stock of New Life Church, in Harrisburg went and had a powerful experience, especially regarding evangelism. He warned me prior to my trip that I would think they didn't understand the gospel invitation so many would accept the invitation. He was right. We saw 454 people commit to Christ for the first time in their lives, 1750 rededicated from backslidden conditions, almost 1200 healed and over 350 go for deliverance. The deliverance ministry only occurred in two of the 16 meetings in 10 days. I did think that they misunderstood the invitation, but they hadn't. The meetings were held in Bogota, Medillin, and Cali. The president of the ministerial alliance in Cali asked me to come back and speak to the pastors in the day and the stadium, which seats 55,000 at night. Dr. Deiros, one of the most respected Baptist scholars and leaders from Argentina and I were planning to work together in Colombia during 1999.

In January 1999, my team met with Pastor Cesar Castellanos. He was born into the Kingdom of God through hearing the audible voice of God, and then experiencing His presence come into his room. His church experiences healings and they have an "encounter weekend" for the new believers where they are taken through inner healing and deliverance, receive the baptism in the Holy Spirit, and the vision for the church. They don't know exactly how many people are in the church at this time; they only count the number of groups not the individuals. He now has a church of 27,000 cell groups that have an average of 10 or more people per group. He and his wife were shot in an assignation attempt. While recuperating for eleven months the church grew by 100,000 while being led by the youth pastor. This is the fastest growing church in the Western Hemisphere. They believe in spiritual warfare through prayer, dancing, praise, fasting, and intercessory prayer. Their services are powerful, and healings usually occur in them. Caesar believes in receiving from the Lord in his prayer life what He wants to occur in the services. They will be meeting three times per Sunday in the coliseum of Bogota.

Central America

In **Guatemala**, the El Shaddai Church, pastored by Harold Cabelleros, now runs over 8,000. It is one of several churches in Guatemala that numbers in the thousands. It is one of the fastest growing churches in the country. It too believes in and practices healing, deliverances, and other demonstrations of God's power, both in the services and in the cell groups. Pastor Harold also believes that the growth of the church is related to the strategic level spiritual warfare that is practiced by selected individuals of the church.

My friend, and fellow evangelist/revivalist, Wes Cambell, has preached for the Catholics in **Mexico** where scores of thousands of Catholics come to a mountain to have open-air meetings led by a Roman Catholic Priest. What brings the thousands to the meetings? The presence of the power of the Holy Spirit demonstrated in signs and wonders.

Drs. Deiros and Mrarida along with Pastor Pablo Bottari (who was the trainer for the deliverance ministry for Evangelist Carlos Annacondia who has led over 3,000,000 people to the Lord this past decade) and me planned to go to **Cuba** in the fall of 1999. We were told by the overseer for Latin America of the Pentecostal Holiness Church in the United States, that the Methodists of Cuba were more Pentecostal than the Pentecostal churches in the United States. He told us that 80% of the Methodists in Cuba were Pentecostal in experience.[76] The meetings will be jointly attended, only by pastors from Methodist, Baptist, and Pentecostal churches.

North America

North America along with Western Europe has long been considered by some to be the Nazareth of the Church world. We are a nation of skeptics, and proud of it. Regardless of which evangelist that I have spoken with, I hear the same report; they do not see the same degree of healing and miracles here that they do in other non-western countries. I long for the day when that is no longer true. Yet, in spite of this, those churches that are open to the presence of God's Spirit and his gifts are growing faster as a whole than those that are not open. But of course, there are exceptions. Though I have been emphasizing the growth of movements as a sign of the ability of the movement to draw people, I realize it does not vindicate the group as an orthodox Christian group. Heresies can grow fast also. The following chart indicates just this truth with the second fastest group being the Mormon cult.

In a study of churches in the U.S. and Canada between 1965 and 1989 the following was reported: Disciples of Christ -45%,

Presbyterian -32%, Episcopal -29%, United Church -21%, United Methodist -19%, Evangelical Lutheran -8%, Roman Catholic 23%, Southern Baptist 38% Church of the Nazarene 63%, Seventh Day Adventist 92%, Assemblies of God (Pentecostal)121%, Mormon 133%, Church of God (Pentecostal)183%[77]

The fastest growth among the North American churches has been the thousands of new Charismatic churches. Apostolic networks numbering thousands of churches have developed over the past twenty years. Most of these networks of churches would embrace the dynamic of power evangelism with its primary focus on healing and deliverance.

Chapter 9

Summary

It is my opinion based upon this study that in most places of the world the Church is growing the fastest where there is openness to, and practice of, power evangelism. I believe that as the world becomes more post-modern in its worldview, those churches that are open to power evangelism will be best suited to influence their communities. The old apologetic, which was entirely based upon presentation evangelism, needs to be augmented by utilizing **power evangelism** within the presentation of the gospel. **Presence evangelism** softens the hearts of the unbelievers, making it easier to be open to the gospel. But in order for us to most effectively reach the masses, especially the masses of the 10/40 window, we also need to embrace **power evangelism's emphasis upon healing and deliverance,** and not be afraid of the phenomena that can accommodate the visitation of God's empowering presence. Power evangelism is on God's heart and is one of the four emphases that the Spirit is saying to the church today.[78]

I believe that God is going to pour out his Spirit in the last days causing one of the most powerful revivals in human history. Perhaps this revival is already happening in parts of the earth. More people are alive right now who have not heard the gospel than have lived and died in the history of humanity. What if Smith Wigglesworth was right when before his death he told Lester Sumrall about a coming revival? Sumrall, who died in 1996, related this experience with Wigglesworth in these words:

> I see it!
> What do you see?
>   I see a revival coming to planet earth, as never before. There will be untold multitudes who will be saved. No man will say, "So many and so

many," because no man will be able to count those who will come to Jesus Christ. *I see it!* The dead will be raised, the arthritic healed, cancer will be healed. No disease will be able to stand before God's people, and it will spread all over the world. It will be a worldwide thrust of God's power and a thrust of God's anointing. I will not see it, but you will see it.[79]

A multitude of lost souls coming into His Kingdom because of the mighty acts of power! Let it be in our day!

It was my intention at the outset of this study to inform you of the mighty outpouring of the Spirit that has happened and that is continuing to happen in our day. I wanted these stories to create in you a thirst to see power evangelism in our day and hour. How hungry are you? How thirsty are you? Do you desire to see more than you've ever seen before? If so, I invite you to join me on this quest for more of the Holy Spirit's outpouring in our time.

Endnotes

(Endnotes)

[1] Daniel Mark Epstein, *Sister Aimee: The Life of Aimee Semple McPherson,* (New York: Harcourt Brace & Company, 1993) pp. 213-213

[2] Owen Jorgensen, *Supernatural: The Life of William Branham, Book Three: The Man and His Commission (1946-1950),* (Tucson, Arizona: Tucson Tabernacle, 1994) p.176

[3] Dr. R. Edward Miller, *Cry for me Argentina:Revival begins in City Bell,* (Essex, England: Sharon Publications Ltd., 1988) pp.42,43,45

[4] This is the opinion of Dr. Pablo Deiros a leading scholar of Latin America, the leading scholar on the history of the protestant church in Argentina. Personal interview 1998.

[5] Oral Roberts, *Expect A Miracle: My Life and Ministry, an Autobiography,* (Nashville, Tennessee: Thomas Nelson Publishers, 1995) p.168

[6] Ibid., p. 161

[7] Ibid., p.135

[8] Lester Sumrall, *Demons The Answer Book,* (Nashville, Tennessee: Thomas Nelson Publishers, 1979) pp. 19-20.

[9] Ibid., p. 24

[10] The whole story is recounted in Lester's Book, *Demons The Answer Book,* (Nashville, Tennessee: Thomas Nelson Publishers, 1979) chapter 1..

[11] Ron Steele, *Plundering Hell-To Populate Heaven: The Reinhard Bonnke Story,* (Melbourne, Florida: Dove Christian Books, 1987) p. 157

[12] David Harrell Jr., *All Things Are Possible: The Healing and Charismatic Revivals in Modern America,* (Bloomington, Indiana: Indiana University Press, 1975) p.94

[13] I heard Dr. Deere teach on this in Evanston in the late 1980's, and it is also the viewpoint in G.B. Caird's book on Revelation.

[14] The Term Third Wave Evangelicals refers to those evangelical which are not dispensational, but who believe all of the gifts of the Holy Spirit are still for the church today. They would distinguish themselves from Classical Pentecostals by not believing that one had to have the **initial evidence** of speaking in tongues.

Neither would they believe that the Baptism in the Holy Spirit **must always** be subsequent to conversion. However, some would be quick to admit that it usually is subsequent to conversion.

[15] For more on this see the works of Dr. C. Peter Wagner, especially Breaking Strongholds in Your City, Confronting the Powers, and Engaging the Enemy; also The Twilight Labyrinth: Why does Spiritual Darkness Linger Where It Does? by George Otis Jr.; and the book which lays down the biblical foundation for fighting the spiritual enemies of God, God at War by Dr. Gregory Boyd. For the other side of this discussion see Three Crucial Questions about Spiritual Warfare by Dr. Clinton E. Arnold.

[16] Acts 19:10-12

[17] Acts 19:26

[18] Acts 19:8-10

[19] Ramsay MacMullen, *Christianizing the Roman Empire (A.D. 100-400)* (New Haven, Connecticut: Yale University. Press, 1984,) p.62

[20] Earle E. Cairnes, *Christianity Through The Centuries* (Grand Rapids, Michigan: Zondervan, 1954, 1967) pp.400-401

[21] D.Partner, Douglas, *Who's Who in Christian History*, ed. Douglas, Comfort, & Mitchell, (Wheaton, Illinois: Tyndale House, 1997, c1992, under "Jonathan Edwards") [an unpaginated electronic work]

[22] Clare George Weakley, Jr. *The Nature of Revival* (Minneapolis, Minnesota: Bethany House Publishers, 1987) p. 79, quoting Nehemiah Curnock, ed., *The Journal of the Reverend John Wesley* (London: Charles H. Kelly, 1909), entry dated March 8, 1739.

[23] Ibid., p. 83, quoting *The Journal of the Reverend John Wesley,* entry dated April 21, 1739.

[24] Ibid., quoting *The Journal of the Reverend John Wesley,* entry dated April 26, 1739.

[25] Ibid., quoting *The Journal of the Reverend John Wesley,* entry dated April 30, 1739.

[26] Ibid., quoting *The Journal of the Reverend John Wesley,* entry dated May 1, 1739.

[27] Ibid., quoting *The Journal of the Reverend John Wesley,* entry dated May 2, 1739.

[28] See my booklet, *Falling Under the Power,* for a study of the biblical, historical, and present accounts of this phenomena. I believe one of the reason the crowds came to Wesley's meetings were the phenomena. God seems to use phenomena as his advertising campaign for revival. That is why the particular phenomena varies from revival to revival.

[29] Clare George Weakley, Jr. *The Nature of Revival* (Minneapolis, Minnesota: Bethany House Publishers, 1987) p. 85-86, quoting *The Journal of the Reverend John Wesley,* entry dated May 2, 1739. See Weakley, p. 138-139 for the account of 26 who manifested demons and some were delivered quoting *The Journal of the Reverend John Wesley,* entry dated June 15, 1739.

[30] Ibid., p. 140, quoting Nehemiah Curnock, ed., *The Journal of the Reverend John Wesley* (London, Charles H. Kelly, 1909), entry dated July 7, 1739

[31] D.Partner, Douglas, *Who's Who in Christian History*, ed. Douglas, Comfort, & Mitchell, (Wheaton, Illinois: Tyndale House, 1997, c1992, under "Jonathan Edwards") [an unpaginated electronic work]

[32] John Havlik and Lewis Drummond, *How Spiritual Awakenings Happen*, (Nashville, Tennessee: The Sunday School Board of the Southern Baptist Convention, 1981) p.15

[33] Peter Cartwright, *Autobiography of Peter Cartwright: With an Introduction, Bibliography and Index by Charles L, Wallis,* (Nashville, Tennessee:, Abingdon Press, 1856) p.45

[34] Global Awakening has just republished this book in its entirety without editing anything out of it. The book was published by the North China Baptist Publishing House. It is the first hand report of one of the Southern Baptist missionaries who experienced the revival, Mary Crawford. In it are many accounts of almost everything that has been characteristic of the Toronto Revival, and the Pensacola Outpouring. It is very sad that few Southern Baptists are not aware of what happened during their greatest revival. Several years ago the book was reprinted by the Southern Baptist, and was edited by Dr. Culpepper. What is interesting was the editing out of almost all of the phenomena of the Holy Spirit. This book should be a gift to all Southern Baptists who desire more of the presence of God in their lives. To order the unedited contact our office. See our website at *www.globalawakening.com* for contact information.

[35] John Havlik and Lewis Drummond, *How Spiritual Awakenings Happen,*

(Nashville, Tennessee: The Sunday School Board of the Southern Baptist Convention, 1981,) Havlik and Drummond, p. 22

[36] Ibid., p.23

[37] Lewis Drummond, *The Awakening That Must Come,* (Nashville, Tennessee: Broadman Press, 1978) p. 17

[38] Notes from my class with Dr. Drummond. I have to admit that Dr. Lewis Drummond had a profound impact and influence upon me to have a great hunger to experience revival.

[39] Paul K. Conkin, *Cane Ridge: America's Pentecost,* (Madison, Wisconsin: The University of Wisconsin Press, 1990) p. 173.

[40] Ibid., p. 19.

[41] Ibid., p. 23

[42] Ibid., p. 24

[43] Ibid., p. 25

[44] Charles L. Wallis, *Autobiography of Peter Cartwright,* (Nashville, Tennessee: Abingdon Press, 1856) p. 12.

[45] Ibid., p. 45

[46] Ibid., p. 46

[47] Ibid., p. 46

[48] See Jack Deere's book, *Surprised by the Voice of God* where he documents how the Reformed denominations removed the prophetic dimension from their earliest writings. I have also mentioned how the Southern Baptist did the same thing in the reprinting of *The Shantung Revival* that had edited almost every supernatural reference to phenomena such as falling, laughing in the Spirit, shaking, feeling electricity going through the body, etc. I have reprinted the book in its entirety and can be purchased by calling 314-416-9239. It is a powerful read of the greatest revival in Southern Baptist history.

[49] Charles L. Wallis, *Autobiography of Peter Cartwright,* (Nashville, Tennessee: Abingdon Press, 1856) p. 46

[50] Ibid., p. 47

[51] See the book, Dr. R. Edward Miller, *Cry for me Argentina:Revival begins in City Bell,* (Essex, England: Sharon Publications Ltd., 1988) pp.42,43,45

[52] We had the leaders come to our church and share with us about the children's experiences in the late 1980's or the early 1990's; I can't remember the exact dates.

[53] Vinson Synan, *The Holiness-Pentecostal Movement In The United States,* (Grand Rapids: Michigan, Wm. B. Erdmans Pub. Company., 1971) p. 24

[54] Ibid., p.25

[55] Charles Finney, *Charles G. Finney: An Autobiography,* (Old Tappan, N.J.: Fleming H. Revell Company, 1876, renewed 1908) pp. 20-21

[56] Ibid., p.21

[57] Ibid., p.180

[58] Ibid., p. 297

[59] Vinson Synan shared this with me at a conference at my church in 1994.

[60] Ibid., p. 86

[61] Ibid., p. 87

[62] Ibid., p. 118 (Italics Martin's)

[63] Ralph Martin, *The Catholic Church at the End of an Age: What is the Spirit Saying?,* (San Francisco, California: Ignatius Press, 1994) pp.30,

[64] Ibid., p. 164

[65] Ibid., pp. 198-199 (Bold emphasis mine)

[66] Harvey Cox, *Fire From Heaven: The Rise of Pentecostal Spirituality and the Reshaping of Religion in the Twenty-First Century,* (New York: Addison-Wesley Publishing Co., 1994) pp. 99-100

[67] Ibid., p. 246

[68] Ibid., p. 246

[69] Ibid., p. 247

[70] Ibid., p. 187

[71] This is based upon an interview I had with Karen Hurston whose father helped pioneer the church with Cho. She said the saints wouldn't have the language of Strategic Level Spiritual Warfare, but they prayed not only to God, but also would direct their declarations to Satan and the demons.

[72] Carolyn Boyd, *The Apostle of Hope: The Dr. Kriengsak Story,* (West Sussex, England: Sovereign World Ltd., 1991) pp. 120-121

[73] Ralph Martin, *The Catholic Church at the End of an Age: What is the Spirit Saying?,* (San Francisco, California: Ignatius Press, 1994) pp. 88-89

[74] Harvey Cox, *Fire From Heaven: The Rise of Pentecostal Spirituality and the Reshaping of Religion in the Twenty-First Century,* (New York: Addison-Wesley Publishing Company, 1994) p. 168

[75] The name for Tommy Tenney's book. It is a must read.

[76] This leader for the Pentecostal Holiness shared this information with me and Dr. Deiros, Mrarida, and Bottari along with Jim Hylton and others at Metro Church in Okalahoma City, Okalahoma in 1998.

[77] Ralph Martin, *The Catholic Church at the End of an Age: What is the Spirit Saying?,* (San Francisco, California: Ignatius Press, 1994) p. 90

[78] Dr. Carlos Mrarida's lecture on Vision given at the Conquering the City For God Conference in 1998 in Florence, Kentucky - for this lecture contact Global Awakening at 717-796-9866. It is one of the most powerful prophetic insights I have heard.

[79] Ron McIntosh, *The Quest For Revival: Experiencing Great Revivals of the Past, Empowering You For God's Move Today!,* (Tulsa, Okalahoma: Harrison House, 1994) pp. 13-14